Street Name Lettering

in the British Isles/Alan Bartram

Lund Humphries, London / Watson-Guptill Publications, New York

Copyright © 1978 Alan Bartram

First edition 1978
Published by
Lund Humphries Publishers Ltd
26 Litchfield Street London WC2

SBN 85331 412 8

First published 1978 in the United States
by Watson-Guptill Publications
a division of Billboard Publications, Inc.
1515 Broadway, New York, N.Y. 10036

ISBN 0–8230–4930–2

Library of Congress Catalog Card Number 78–52296

Designed by Alan Bartram
Made and printed in Great Britain
by W & J Mackay Ltd, Chatham, Kent

Street Name Lettering

This book examines a small-scale object which we see every day without realising how vital it is. Not only would we literally be lost without street names, but they can be a source of pleasure or interest in themselves. They may have an historical interest, giving us information about the area when no other evidence remains – Artesian Road, where formerly there was an artesian well; Observatory Road, on the site of an observatory; Portobello Road, winding down between a series of regularly laid-out streets, originally the track to Portobello Farm; Notting Hill Gate, where the turnpike was – all districts have their history partly recorded by street names. The name might also reflect the time the road was built – Nelson Place, Nile Street. Or it might commemorate a local celebrity; and so on.

But this book is not particularly concerned with such historical associations or allusions. It is mainly about the letterforms used for naming the streets, and the methods of displaying these names. It attempts to show the variations possible, and also tries to show that these small taken-for-granted signs can be exploited to provide not only visual (and historical) interest, but to create a sense of place, of neighbourhood, for our townscapes; that they can help to provide a town with its sense of identity.

There are some signposting situations where the over-riding requirement is legibility, and all other considerations are of secondary importance: directional signs on motor-ways and main roads are examples. But the signs in this book are for roads where people live, or work, or buy their daily needs; and whilst legibility is important, it is not of such exclusive concern that other factors need be sacrificed to it. The man in the motor-car should be borne in mind, but he must not dictate the kind of lettering used, nor the

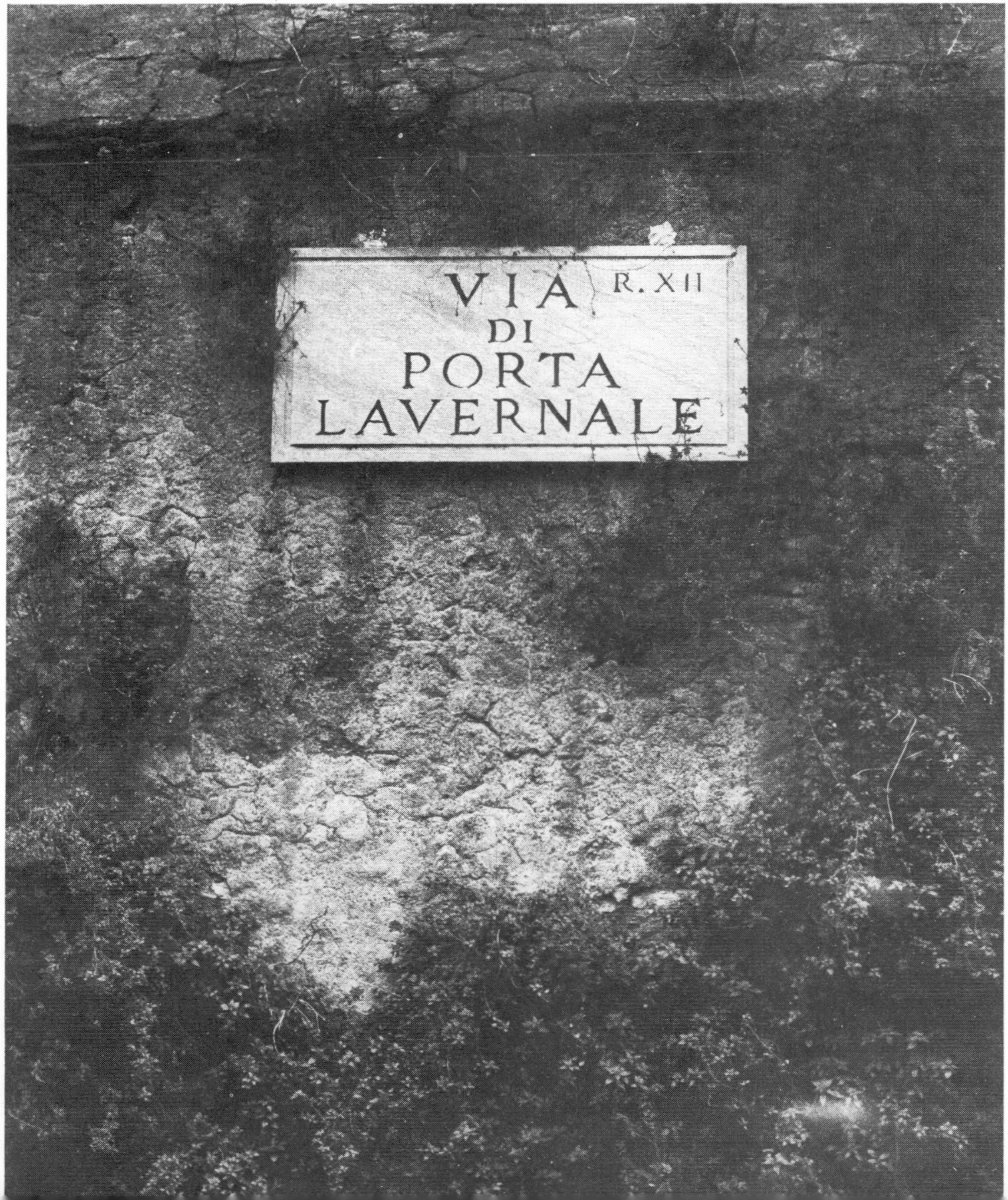

1

Two names from Rome (1) and (2) show the style universally adopted throughout that city, differing only in that names for more important places have richer borders. Cut in marble slabs, the letterforms are undistinguished. Where there is no convenient wall, they are erected on a single tall, slim pole, so that, as with Italian road signs, the structure is unobtrusive, done with visual economy. Unlike ours.

R. PIAZZA II
DEL
QUIRINALE

way it is used. Most of the examples here were put up before mechanical transport was developed, but they still serve their purpose today, whilst adding humanity, richness and subtlety to the townscape.

· Letterforms are amazingly versatile. All kinds of distortions and liberties may be taken with them without destroying their meaning. We all know what an O looks like: it is a circle. But it is also possible for a rectangle, or a square, or a solid square with a fine line in the middle of it, to look like an O. Each letter has an archetypal model from which all letter design starts, but what does this vital archetype look like? It is merely an idea in the mind of man – western man. This subject requires a book of its own; here I can only mention it and pass on. What is important to the present subject is that letterforms can be manipulated to be not only legible, but to lend a special character to an area. They can reflect their environment, draw inspiration from it and, in return, enhance it. They can be given a warm, friendly feeling which helps to make the road they name, and in which one lives, look a personal place with its own flavour; or they can be given a character which makes the words they form look cool, aloof, or hostile. Small-scale items they may be, but street names are pervasive. Their continual presence, which we must always be consulting when walking around a town, especially a strange one, is bound, through the lettering, to have an effect. If the reader disbelieves this, he should walk around Bath.

To say a letterform should be functional is a very vague statement. What does one mean by function? Lettering can be legible, but yet not fully functional; for fitness of purpose, I believe, also implies fitness for its situation.

Street names should not only be sufficiently clear, but also respectful of their environment. The best ones, at Bath, might even be criticised (but not by me) as allowing environmental considerations to detract from their informative function. I believe street names should, ideally, reflect the town's character, or its sense of civic pride, or its sense of identity and community, or all of these. What simpler way, for instance, of telling the passer-by he has left Kensington and is now in Westminster, than by a change in the style of the street name plates?

The letterforms shown in the illustrations are mainly of the four basic families: english, clarendon, egyptian, or grotesque. For clarity's sake, bizarre letterforms are unsuitable; but within these four styles alone, great variations and personal interpretations are possible. A properly-trained signwriter or lettering artist can easily create a legible, individual style for a town, either by designing an alphabet to be used invariably without modification, or by designing a basic form upon which variations can be played.

For the naming of their streets, certain towns have at some stage attempted to create a town style, and evidence of this can often be seen in (undeveloped) central areas, whereas in the later outskirts mediocrity and inconsistency have taken over. No town in Britain has anything approaching the consistency of Rome, where every street, alley or piazza, including recent suburbs, has its name, in a somewhat inert roman letter, cut in a rectangular marble slab. In England, Cambridge has a clarendon of distinctive design, cast in metal, scattered around the town; Oxford has a somewhat similar style, and another, sturdier letter. This letterform can be seen, with variations, in many towns, although never exclusively. Throughout much of Hampstead, a clarendon on ceramic tiles is found extensively, effectively embedded in beautiful old red brick walls; the same form and tile can be seen in Colchester, Portsmouth, and elsewhere. Several London boroughs have a fairly consistent approach to the naming of their streets: Westminster has throughout recently erected practical if unexciting enamelled signs in two versions of Univers capitals.

None of these is particularly adventurous, although many are pleasing enough. If they are made too beautiful, they get stolen; even Westminster signs get stolen. But one town has a quite remarkable collection of (unstealable) street names, and that is Bath. Here is a uniformity that for me is the best kind of all – a uniformity of feeling, which is given richness and interest by having hardly two names in exactly the same style.

Whenever I visit Bath, I am surprised by the scale of these names. Cut in stone, usually on the string course of the building, the letters are often nine inches high or more. They range from english letters, through moderns and clarendons, to grotesques (I have not found any egyptians). The majority were probably cut by one mason or group of masons, and are not necessarily contemporary with the buildings. The cutting was spread over a long enough period to show the development of the classic letter, and its decline. Many have been re-cut in recent years, the best of the old forms being faithfully followed.

Although large in scale, they fit their situation perfectly because they are truly part of the building. If they had consisted of enamelled plates screwed onto the building, their effect would have been less pleasing, and possibly sometimes destructive. Even painting-in the cut, as has been done with some names, needs to be done very sensitively for it not to be damaging.

These Bath street names are a perfect match for a town which, until the 1960s, was a visually civilised, unmarred environment. They demonstrate that a uniformity of treatment and some consistency of feeling is enough to bind a variety of styles into a coherent whole. Too often, a style is achieved the easy but unimaginative way, by clamping all lettering into one rigid formula. But lettering is a living thing, and much is gained by treating it as such.

One must be practical, and admit that few towns today could treat every street name as an individual problem in the way Bath has. It can be argued that the majority of street names for any one town can be handled in a fairly standardised way, although the positioning of each requires individual consideration. But there will always be a sizeable number demanding their own unique solution, both for their letterform and their technique, and especially for their siting. The challenge is to create a sufficiently versatile scheme which can cope with a variety of situations, allowing considerable freedom within the scheme, yet achieving a visual identity overall. I see no reason why the technique cannot be varied for certain situations, if the variety of building styles requires this. Bath was fortunate in having solely stone buildings, all built in a style which was basically similar, and this allowed a uniform technique of cut letters (with occasional painted letters which could well have been cut). No other English town is as homogeneous as Bath was before 1965. So each town demands its own solution, which can only be devised by someone who knows, understands, and has a feeling for that town. A large town or city, however, would be best treated as a series of separate

One occasionally sees plates defining wards of a town. Such administrative divisions do not always correspond to the true neighbourhood divisions. (3) shows not only a ward plate and a fire hydrant plate, both in cast iron with a clarendon letterform (and recently repainted a beautiful blue), but also a banal enamelled street name of a form commonly found throughout the City. A pity it is so characterless. (4) is from Clonmel, Co. Tipperary. Also in cast iron, the letterform is unusual for this material, being a modern, with its sudden contrasts between thick strokes and thin. In this example, the difference is so extreme it is known as a fat face.

WEST
WARD

Nº 5
B.B
J.HACKETT
MAYOR
1843

neighbourhoods; for instead of attempting to weld a moderate-sized community into a whole, here the problem is to break down a large, possibly amorphous, urban area into smaller neighbourhoods with which people can associate. London is the prime example, not only because of its size, and its own division into boroughs, but because historically it is a conglomeration of individual villages, and still retains this character, with its various High Streets and clearly differentiated centres. It is just such historical facts that architects, designers, and signwriters, ought to be pointing up in their work (how few do!). Even Edinburgh, with its old centre and Georgian New Town, or Dublin with its Georgian area and its other areas, would clearly require several variations of treatment. Such 'awkward-nesses' should be accepted as an incentive to the imagina-tion, not as obstacles, and certainly should not be ignored.

Few towns are suitable for carved street names, although carved slate slabs would suit many of our northern, Cornish or Welsh towns. But one can visualise, for instance, signs painted on wooden boards, executed by a team of signwriters, for which the letters might be given some, perhaps considerable, variety, whilst still, by con-tinuity of colour, or general effect, achieving a family likeness. They might require more maintenance than the normal enamelled signs, cast-iron signs, or ceramic letters; but it would be interesting to compare the costs. And as any considerable and permanent reduction in unemploy-ment in this country seems unlikely, there might be worse ways of providing jobs for young people than by deliber-ately creating signwriting and lettering work, after proper training. Better than unemployment benefit. The realisation and acceptance of such a situation could provide remark-able opportunities for the crafts generally – among them signwriting; opportunities which would flow with the tide of increasing interest in what used to be thought of as the dying crafts.

Many New Towns, particularly in Scotland, have an official post of Town Artist. Here, too, is another opportunity. 'The broad objective . . . is to increase the accessibility and participation in art to all sections of the community . . . the Artist should be able to communicate his/her art to a wide range of people and work closely with many different groups and individuals.' Ways of improving the environment are often part of the Town Artist's brief. In effect, it is simply providing imagination for the solution of constructional or functional problems; or, as one of them describes it, to be the aesthetic conscience of the town. Frequently the result is delight instead of brutality or banality – at minimal extra cost. What more pertinent and all-pervasive field for providing small-scale visual pleasure and a sense of identity than that of street names? I have mentioned signwriting as a technical solution but, especially for a New Town, far more imaginative solutions could be developed (or simple ones too: one Italian town – I thought Venice, but it seems not – has, throughout, black stencilled letters on a white ground). Ceramic tiles are one existing form which could be developed creatively. Their advantage is that they can be happily integrated into their surroundings (as can be seen at Hampstead). Cast concrete letters are another possibility, and a little imagina-tive thinking can easily suggest further techniques. In the case of a New Town, street names could be as truly integrated with buildings or surroundings as at Bath, and could become important decorative features at selected

*The cast–iron street name in (**6**) is of a style frequently found in Cambridge. The Ls have an odd, characteristic tuck–in. Initial letters in this style are always larger than the rest.*

Oxford has several series of cast-iron street names, some in a clarendon rather similar to (6). *A fatter and more condensed clarendon is also frequently found (**7**). The plate border is more elaborate than those at Cambridge.*

7

Anyone who has visited Hampstead will be familiar with this style (8). Not, unfortunately, universally used there, it is nonetheless widespread. A most characteristic effect is created by the black-and-white ceramic tiles embedded in old richly-red brick walls. One of the most identity-creating combinations I know; a supreme example of what this book is about.

major thoroughfare junctions, especially pedestrian ways. Approached as sculpture, but with a purpose, they really could communicate at various levels to 'a wide range of people'.

Why such a fuss about street names – yet alone a whole book? It seems to me that anything which can help to carve up anonymous conglomerations of buildings into small neighbourhoods with which one can identify, is worthwhile. When Nicolete Gray wrote *Lettering on Buildings* in 1960, it was enough, in her section on street names, to suggest that they should be, firstly, legible, and secondly, preferably of good letterforms – 'a pleasure to the inhabitant as well as a convenience to strangers'. Today we know this is not quite enough. With the wholesale destruction of English town centres, and the replacement of local character by all-purpose, no-place banality, we are aware of how much we took for granted, now that it is gone. It is not right that we can travel fifty miles, or two hundred and fifty miles, and find something virtually identical to the place we left – the same style of building, the same language of planning, the same materials, the same street furniture, the same signs, the same lettering – and the same street names. It is not in human nature to feel that this is progress.

Bureaucracy, however well-intentioned, can be so clumsy. Even costed at the primary level, so much standardisation, done in the cause of economy and efficiency, turns out to be more expensive than small, localised solutions. The cost in terms of distress and reduction of a society by the remoteness and anonymity of decisions is incalculable.

I happen to live in a district with which I can identify closely, in spite of it being in London. I can approach it as if peeling off layers on an onion. Leaving the busy shopping and business area (buses, taxis, jumbled-up traffic, and tourists burdened with Marks & Spencer bags), I cycle across Edgware Road and enter a more open, quieter (though still car- and taxi-infested) residential area. Peeling off that layer, I pass near Paddington Station, and come to Bayswater (package-tour hotels and enormous intrusive coaches). Through peaceful residential areas (very little traffic now) I enter my demesne, or my manor, as the police would describe it, around which is a sort of psychological fence. Through that layer, down the top end of Portobello Road (memories of it being described as a farm track winding through fields), I arrive at my road, which runs alongside a large communal garden – the centre of my onion. All this to me is of great importance, although I am not claiming everyone would feel this way. I am sure this sort of situation cannot be consciously created with some kind of instant neighbourhood pack, but I very much believe it is worth trying to assist its development. I also believe that lettering and street names can be used as a minute part of this attempt. In theory, if a broad conception is correct, details don't matter. In practice, as far as environment is concerned, it seems they do matter. It all matters, right down to the tiniest detail, down to the little plants growing up between the garden paving stones.

These four pictures illustrate the four main styles of letterforms used in British street names.

(9) English: *this is a term I use to describe a style forming a very large part of the English vernacular tradition. It differs from the classic roman letter, such as Bembo in which this book is set, by having a more extreme difference between thick and thin strokes, the change between the two also being sharper. The stress – that is, the angle of the thick parts of circular letters – is vertical. Serifs are pointed, bracketed – the stroke flows into them – and horizontal (even in the lower-case letters which do not appear in this book). Proportions of letters relative to each other are a little different from the roman.*

This example is from Bath, Somerset.

(10) Clarendon: *fundamentally this is a bold english letter. Proportions of letters relative to each other are similar, but it may be found in condensed or expanded forms. Weights can also vary; it is usually quite bold, as in this example. Serifs flow, bracketed, from the strokes, but end bluntly. It is a form much used for casting, and suits that technique admirably.*

This example is from Wellington, Somerset.

9

10

(11) Egyptian: *relative proportions of this letter are again the same, but it is normally a heavier letter. The main characteristic is the slab serif – a rectangular, square-cut termination which has no bracketing. Rather a powerful letter, and frequently the strokes are of more or less even weight. Very bold weights, however, necessitate more variation to retain legibility, and the result is often a very rich form.*

This example is from Crediton, Devon.

(12) Grotesque: *in reality, an egyptian without serifs. Capable of being adapted to extreme differences of weight, the remarks made about egyptians apply here too.*

This example is from Bath, Somerset. The angularity here is a frequent characteristic, but not invariable.

11

12

The earliest surviving street names seem to have been cut in stone. Overwhelmed by this unhappy sequence from Grantham, Lincolnshire (**13**), the one decent piece of lettering faintly visible was probably done in the late eighteenth century. It has strong echoes of the slate tombstones of this period, for which the area is noted.

Also cut in stone is this name from Kingsbridge, Devon (14). Even today, some architects allow for street names to be incorporated coherently into their design: a small and simple gesture which might well be made more often. Without such provision, ill-conceived and ill-placed street furniture can turn a basically good scheme into a mess.

Two more names cut into the building itself: an egyptian from Colne, Lancashire (**15**), and an english letter from Carlisle, Cumberland (**16**). The stone slab of (15) is well-incorporated into the wall; but the existence of a string course, such as seen in (16), is a gift for perfectly relating the name to both building and street. Both examples look as if they could be part of a more widespread scheme, but this does not appear to be the case.

15

16

A rich, well-drawn clarendon, probably cast in plaster,
has a unity with the stuccoed wall at Hull, Yorkshire (**17**).
The lack of upkeep evident here need not condemn this
solution.

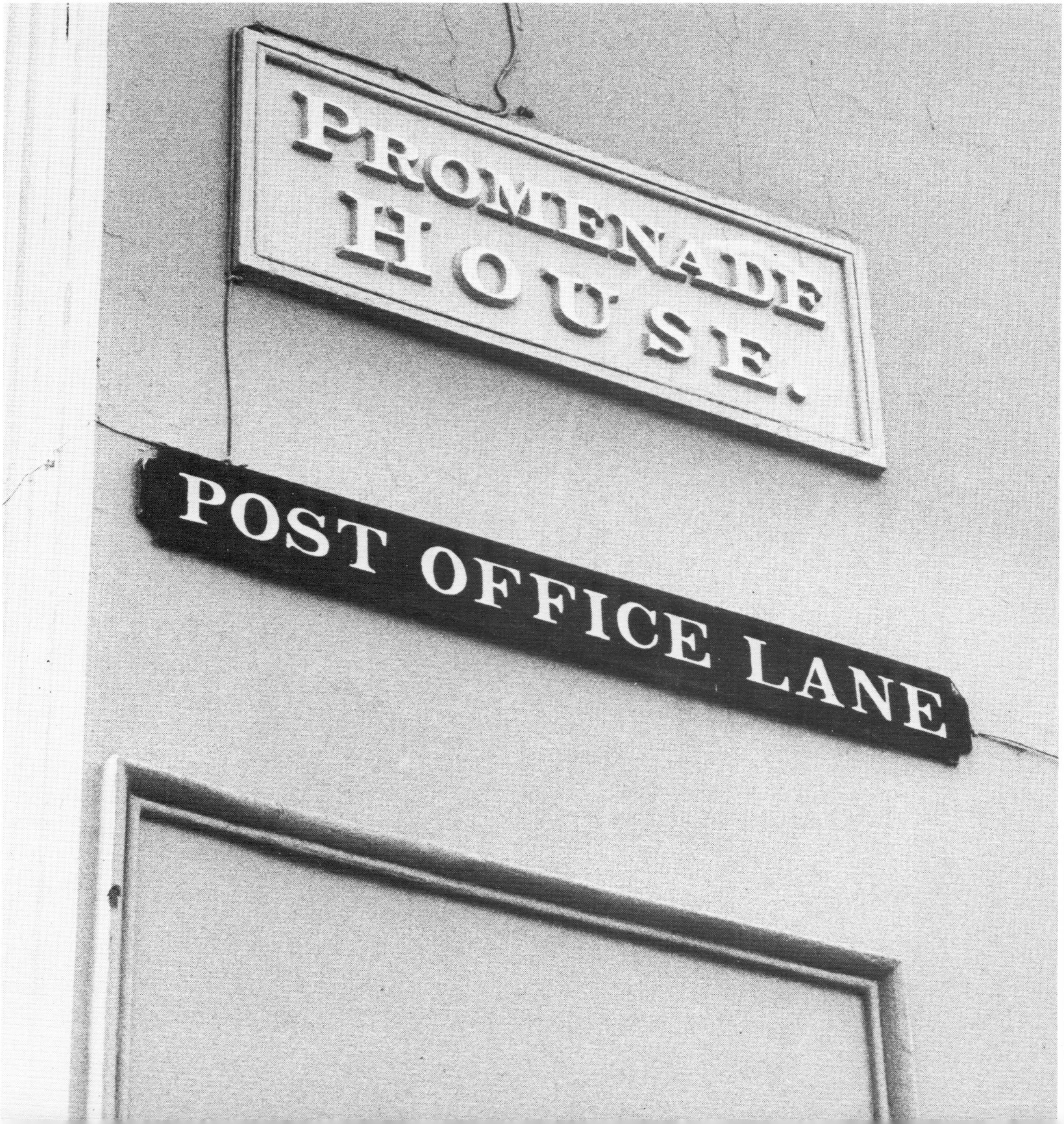
PROMENADE
HOUSE.
POST OFFICE LANE

Two more good cast clarendons, this time at Cheltenham, Gloucestershire (**18**). The upper one is probably plaster, the lower one cast iron. A neater relationship with the architectural detail could have been achieved with little effort.

A slightly lighter, more even-weight, clarendon than the previous examples is a sole example, in cast iron, seen at Tamworth, Staffordshire (**19**). Most of these cast-iron plates probably date from the second half of the nineteenth century; some might be of the first or second decade of the twentieth.

(**20**) shows the style of street name commonly found in the centre of Great Torrington, Devon; and (**21**) is yet another clarendon in cast iron, at Waterford, Ireland. The name roughly dates this one! The amount of letterspacing can often affect the appearance to an unexpected degree: these two forms are very similar, but not the effect.

20

21

A clarendon at Tenby, Pembrokeshire (**22**) has a rounded
look, possibly due to layers of paint applied over the years.
At Wellington, Somerset (**23**), the form is slightly condensed.

   Subtleties such as whether the plate is recessed, or
attached to the surface, are visually important.

22

23

(24) is from Bath, Somerset; (25) from Bolton, Lancashire.
In the latter, 1 has been used instead of I; was this an
attempt to improve the spacing? I am not sure it was a
good idea.

Two from Uckfield, Sussex, (**26**) and (**27**), use a clarendon with smaller serifs and a greater, sharper, contrast between thicks and thins.

An idiosyncratic clarendon is found throughout much of Cambridge (**28**); the same style can be seen in (6). Another clarendon is also found there (**29**), unusually closely spaced to pleasing effect. The borders of both styles are particularly simple.

Spacing, tightness within the borders of the plate, the form of the border: small details like these need careful consideration. The third dimension created by the casting process achieves a richness missing from enamelled plates, and creates a visual interplay with a textured background such as these brick walls.

Two more from Cambridge: (**30**) is unusually light in
weight, an english letter; (**31**) is similar to (29) – apparent
minute differences could be due to a combination of casting
factors and repainting over the years.

30

31

Two from Oxford (**32**) and (**33**), the former rather similar
to the Cambridge letter (28).

32

33

A name from Exeter (**34**) has good, strong, sharply-cast egyptian letters with a simple surround. The form is identical with (**11**) from nearby Crediton; clearly the product of the same foundry. Another example of contrasting yet sympathetic textures.

Cheltenham, Gloucestershire, has several names using this egyptian form (**35**) and (**36**). Unlike all the cast letters so far, this is not in relief, but impressed into the surface.

35

36

The egyptian letters from Wragby, Lincolnshire (**37**) are bolder and richer than the previous examples, while (**38**) from South Molton, Devon, has lighter letters, a little weaker in form.

Two plates with fairly even-weight egyptians, and one plate with a grotesque and Irish half-uncials: Cork, Ireland (**39**).

Also from Cork, the cast-iron form relates happily with the cast-iron railings (40). So could cast concrete letters relate to today's concrete buildings.

This nameplate from Bristol (**41**), rather the worse for wear, like most of that city, is, except for the Es, in the same style as our Cheltenham examples (35) and (36). A final cast-iron plate, from South Molton, Devon (**42**), is an unusual condensed clarendon.

For the first half of the twentieth century, the cast-iron plate was probably the most common form of street name. These examples, however, usually use a commonplace grotesque letter and are not shown here.

A unique letter, I imagine, is this cast plaster plaque at Chatham, Kent (**43**). It has a naïve, slightly incompetent charm.

The most common form of street name used in Britain now is the enamelled plate. I show very few, since the letterforms are usually lacking interest. We shall see a typical example later; here is an earlier (and better) form, in blue and white, almost French in character, from Lewes, Sussex (**44**).

The really upsetting thing about the present enamelled plates being put up is that good rich forms, as seen here, would not cost a penny more. Compare this form (**44**) with the enamelled one in (**59**), which is used throughout the country.

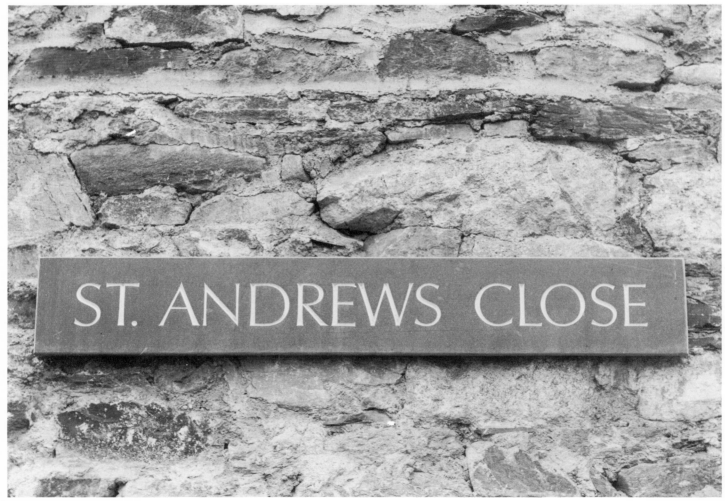

A form with immense possibilities, as yet unexploited, is the carved slate slab. Here are two, (**45**) from Ashburton, Devon, and (**46**) from Truro, Cornwall; the latter looks as if it could be a trial for more extensive use throughout the city. I only wish the letterform in both was more exciting. At Ashburton, it is an indeterminate sans with incipient serifs – or perhaps a roman with vestigial serifs. The Truro form is definitely a roman, slightly and pleasingly angular. But it could be better yet.

Although the cutting of slate slabs is initially more laborious than producing printed and enamelled signs, they should last for several centuries, pollution permitting. The great advantage, which should be leapt at, is that each name can be a new design in itself.

Two names on a larger scale. At Brighton, Sussex, (47) is a clumsy egyptian. It is not really very nice here, but the idea has possibilities. At Liverpool, Lancashire, (48) has a large, good, probably wooden clarendon, gilded.

This splendid little name at Modbury, Devon (**49**) and (**50**), presumably cast, in generous relief, in plaster, creates an effect quite disproportionate to its small size. A rather well-designed grotesque, it demonstrates how a simple device can enliven a whole wall, and how street names can be an asset, not a bothersome necessity.

KING WILLIAM S?

London's West Strand development of the 1830s, planned by Nash and executed by Smirke, includes as part of its design the street names on all sides. Those in the pictures (**51**) and (**52**) are in an egyptian; although oddly the numbers 449 visible on the extreme right of (52) are in a condensed clarendon, while the word 'Strand' there, and 'West Strand' elsewhere, are in a clarendon barely distinguishable from the egyptians, except for a slightly lighter weight of letter and bracketed serifs.

The whole block is in process of extensive rebuilding, but most of Smirke's surviving exterior is being restored to its original form, purged of accretions; we hope the lettering, too, survives.

Another example, again in egyptian form, of street names incorporated into the architectural design, can be found at Newcastle-upon-Tyne (**53**). It dates from 1830. It is as effective on these grand buildings as the similarly-cast letter is on the simple terrace house in (49).

I am cheating here by including an address not a street name; but this London example (**54**) shows another possible technique using metal letters. Individual letters like these present more problems of erection than complete name plates, but the extra trouble can pay off, as here.

In several of their estates, the Greater London Council have used ceramic-tiled letters inset in walls, in the Hampstead style (8). This one is at Stepney (**55**). It looks less good, somehow, in two lines; but the insetting is pleasing. It should be vandal-proof; even paint-spray proof, if sufficiently high up on the wall. The letterform is not quite the same as at Hampstead.

It might be a good idea, in the making of such tiles, to position the letter nearer the top of the tile than the bottom, or else to use an equivalent of the nick on printers' type; then such mistakes as upside-down Ns and Ss could be avoided more easily.

Ceramic tiles using a different letterform – more english than clarendon – can be seen at Newton Abbot, Devon, (56) and (57). White letters are on a blue background (of varied tone, as can be seen; I find this more attractive than distracting).

It really is a *very* good technique, and one which allows great freedom of letterform and of colour. Think what Italians could do with it. And its subtleties of texture and colour make up for the lack of strongly three-dimensional form.

An interesting alternative to ceramic tiles would be to cast individual letters in relief – in concrete, for instance – on a tile base.

56

57

Clarendons on ceramic tiles (I don't know why it is usually a clarendon) can be found in Colchester, Portsmouth, and elsewhere. They are widely used at Ilfracombe, Devon, as seen in the next five pictures. The form is very slightly different from either the Hampstead or the Stepney examples (8) and (55); it is the best of the three. Tiles are blue; (58) is on a white-painted wall.

It is difficult at times to enter into the official mind. Just what did they think they were achieving, whoever it was that put up this dispiriting enamelled sign (**59**), with its sluggish letterform and malformed stumps for serifs.

   And do such signs come in sets, with poles complete? Why not just screw it onto the wall, for heaven's sake?

Two more examples from Ilfracombe, (**60**) and (**61**).

A variation on the standard blue-and-white tile at Ilfracombe is this one in black and gold (**62**) – presumably to acknowledge the importance of the street concerned. Variations to mark such features are an idea well worth developing: even such simple devices as inlines, outlines, shadows and so on, to enrich the same basic form, would be effective.

A final tile, from Barnstaple, Devon, (63) is an unusual decorative letter, white on blue, used intermittently throughout the town. The S is upside down.

The rest of the pictures are of Bath, about which city I have already talked in the introduction. I make no apologies for including so many: that is the point of Bath street names; and although the end of my book, Bath was also its beginning, the starting-off point, the place which made me realise how important street names could be.

The nature of the Bath street names grew naturally from the material of the buildings; the fact that it was easily worked; and the design of the buildings, allowing consistent positioning. The letterforms mainly used are consistent in time and in spirit with the architecture; even the later grotesques, being used normally for the streets of artisan houses, relate to them.

If each particular problem were given its particular solution, our towns could gain in character.

I start with a general view (**64**). This is from the Circus.

The majority of the Bath names are cut in an english letter, but variations on the basic form occur almost everywhere. This exploits the technique of individually cutting each name by hand, instead of using some more mechanised system. A recutting of one of the most accomplished forms is seen in (**65**).

Two very similar styles are seen in (**66**) and (**67**); the Rs and
Es are slightly different.

66

67

A close-up of (**68**) can be seen in (9).

The strokes in (69) and (70) are of more even weight than many of these Bath examples, and the letters are of a very regular proportion.

The serifs in (71) are small; whilst they are unusually strong, almost like a clarendon, in (72). The road is no longer named Church Street, and this name had previously been obscured by a board screwed down over it; but fortunately someone (the house owner?) has removed this to reveal a well-preserved example of original cutting.

69

70

71

72

There is no way of dating the names; most appear to date from the late eighteenth to early nineteenth century. (**73**), (**74**) and possibly (**75**), seem the original cutting; (**76**) has been recut. This recutting, wherever it occurs, has been done with great skill; in fact, one gets the impression that the recut letters are of considerably better quality than many of the originals. Lettercutters cannot be much blamed for the paucity of good lettercutting today.

73

74

75

76

One wonders at the duplication, but it is far less offensive here (**77**) than the example in (59). Perhaps the original cut letter had decayed badly, and the painted sign replaced it until the later recutting.

The form is very similar to that seen in (66), with its quirky R; but the letterspacing is closer.

This recutting takes an unusual form with long triangular serifs (**78**).

Was the little 'e' a correction, or the original intention (**79**)?
I like to think the former, a mistake turned to happy
effect.

As I have already said, until the 1960s Bath was a visually civilised place. Maybe it wasn't such a good idea to split the name in (80) either side of the drainpipe, but what sort of mind is it that feels the need for the addition? Worse, these commonplace plates, green and white versions of (59), are spreading like the pox around large areas of Bath.

The mind (that is, the City Corporation) which can allow these signs in Bath is the mind which can allow – which has systematically planned – the destruction of a unique city. Little things are symptomatic of larger ills.

And yet someone must have commissioned the recutting. The same Bath Corporation, perhaps?

(**81**) shows a mixture of upright and italic I have not seen elsewhere in Bath; the scale of this particular name is also unusually large.

Two slightly different styles for different parts of the street (**83**), (**84**).

Some streets have a different style for each appearance of
the name, as at Alfred Street. (86) and (87) show only two
forms; (87) has the long triangular serifs we saw in (78).

86

87

Both (**88**) and (**89**), although different, have extreme variations between thick and thin strokes – almost a modern.

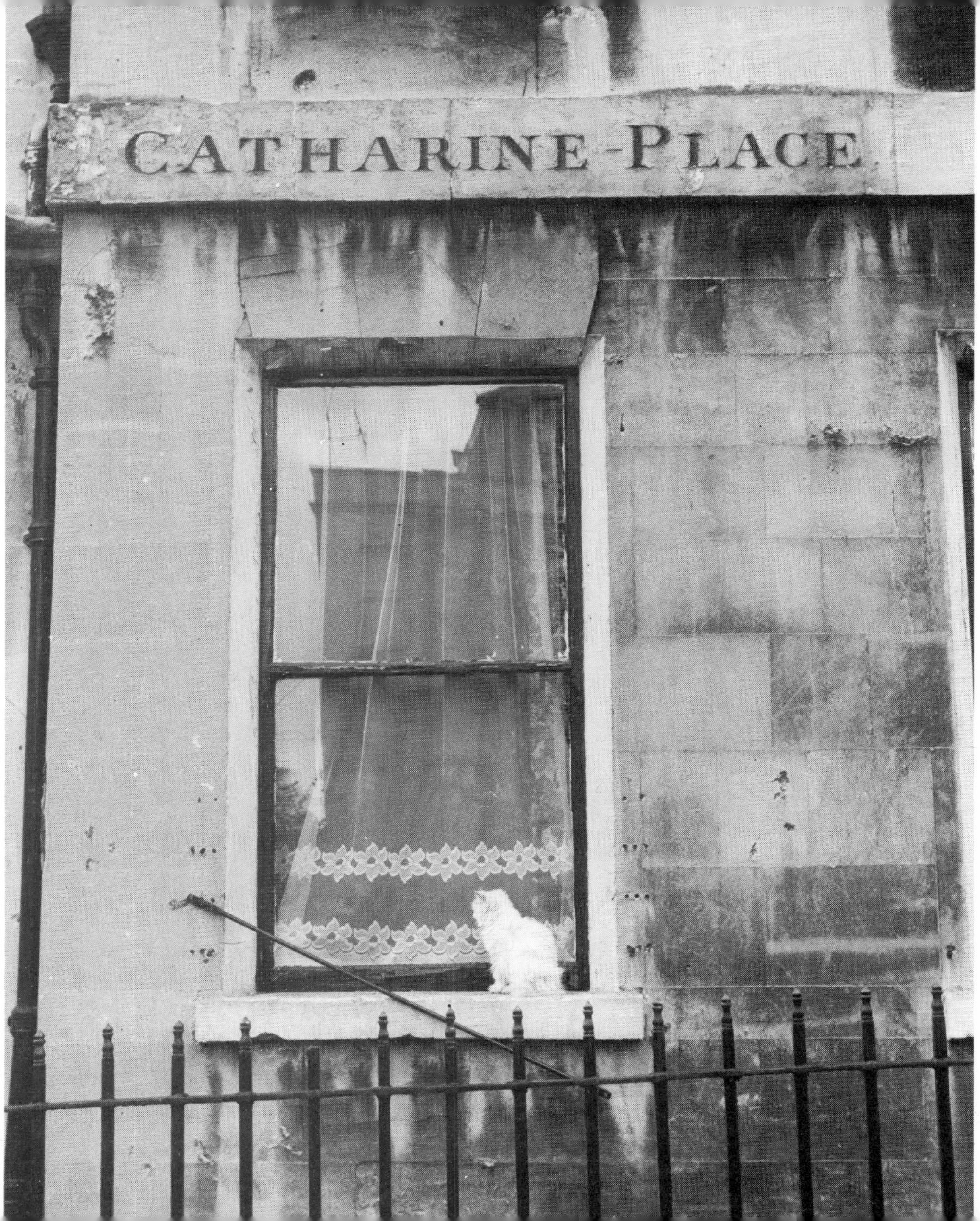
CATHARINE-PLACE

Two similar letterforms in the Bathwick area, (**90**) and (**91**):
a little more spidery, perhaps a little later.

Another example of different form at Bathwick, (**92**) and (**93**). A particularly large-scale letter; too big, perhaps.

Two moderns, (**94**) and (**95**), with their lack of bracketing and a sharp difference between thicks and thins. Not as rich and satisfying a form as the english letter, it is akin to the engravers' lettering of the period. (94) is somewhat unskilled in its cutting.

94

Three rather coarser letters: (**96**), like a rather crude engraver's letter; (**97**), which is almost a clarendon; and (**98**), which has increased enough in weight to become a clarendon.

In some of the humbler parts of Bath, grotesques are used, as here (**99**). This one can be seen in close-up in (12).

96

97

98

100

101

Many of these areas contain the artisan-type dwellings which the Corporation is so keen to destroy. In (**102**) the style of these buildings can be seen; house numbers are also incised, in a form matching the name.

Many of these grotesques have a pleasing, architectural, angularity. (**103**) is carved, (**104**) painted.

Another painted version (**105**), more expanded, and bolder, than the previous one.

The end of the line (**106**). The style of building on which this example appears can be seen in the distance in (102).

Bath is Bath. It is far from my intention to suggest that all towns should have similar lettering carved into their buildings. But I do suggest that the principle – using a wide variety of excellent and related forms in a consistent way – could be followed. There could be a regular format and colour of plaques, for instance, but the letterforms themselves, carved, signwritten, cast, or whatever, need have no particular consistency. A team of good signwriters should be allowed – encouraged – to use their imaginations and whims of the moment, just as in Bath. Whether the technique – carving, painting, and so on – should be constant depends, I think, upon such factors as the size of the town and its architectural character.

For national road signs, consistency is I suppose desirable. Britain is such a richly varied country that to try to reflect its character changes would only lead to confusion; we shall have to content ourselves with the change in the character of the town names themselves (the Middle Wallops, the Aysgarths), and the evocative if unpronounce-able ones of Wales. But names of streets are on the whole far less characteristic of their locality than names of towns; exactly the same ones appear almost everywhere. I would hate to see the Ministry of Transport lettering, excellent though it is, used for them throughout the country: street names and road signs serve quite different purposes, even though there is an overlap. Most of the enamelled street names in present use employ a far inferior letter than the MoT form; *and* they are used throughout the country. What is acceptable in a brick-built area cannot be right in an area of hard northern stone.

Having in Britain disastrously welded areas of local government into larger units, we have learnt the hard way that bigger is not more beautiful. We need to break down those units into humanly-acceptable areas: man-sized, and woman- and child-sized areas, with a sense of place and locality. People are not automata, not yet. They still have their irrational needs, they are strange beyond belief. To be able to identify with something outside themselves, but graspable – whether an idea, a creed, a society, or a neighbourhood – seems to be a necessity for many, perhaps most, people. There can be a kind of pleasure, a reassurance, in returning home from a journey and recognising the familiar landmarks, the style of building, a particular combination of houses, streets and trees, perhaps – and a style of street names peculiar to that place.